Reflections in Nature

Reflections in Nature

MARTIN NORMAN

RESOURCE *Publications* · Eugene, Oregon

REFLECTIONS IN NATURE

Resource Publications
An Imprint of Wipf and Stock Publishers
199 W. 8th Ave., Suite 3
Eugene, OR 97401

www.wipfandstock.com

PAPERBACK ISBN: 978-1-7252-6876-0
HARDCOVER ISBN: 978-1-7252-6875-3
EBOOK ISBN: 978-1-7252-6877-7

08/03/21

This book is dedicated to my mother who loved nature and it's sounds and showed such love and kindness to us all.

Contents

The Solitary Orange Drink!

The solitary orange drink stands alone on the deserted
picnic table, suddenly abandoned before the sweeping
rain, overlooking the pebble grey beach, without even a
seagull to distract, whilst the distant mist encroaches, hiding
the elusive coast, as we gaze on something interrupted
which we have missed, like the haunting Mary Celeste,
leaving us to ponder: Are we half empty or half full?

The Skylark

Skylark, rising and rising in hope, your song undimmed,
As your sound splendors above the hilltops green,
Reaching deeper, sharing joy, as wingtips beat with
Seemingly endless Purpose,
Your inspiration to reach all we fear!

Companionship!

Resting, motionless, across estuary fair, the stillness
in the air, stimulating a sense of profound change,
whilst the mallard ducks sit closely side by side—in
contrast to us—looking outwards with an ambience of
quiet contentment, their beaks moving in perfect
symmetry, to the left and then to the right, whilst
balancing on the hotel wall, as if replacing human
presence; their eyes resting over the calm water
below, now undisturbed, little to infringe, conveying
a message whilst safe and secure!

The Road to Nowhere!

Silent Street we walk in, with sparkling Christmas
Lights, glowing gloriously to the mystery of darkness, no
Bustling purpose of human activity, bar a distant haunting
Shout, everyone asleep whilst golden bulbs display overhead
Their warmth and comfort, to the harsh reality of absence,
On the empty road to nowhere!

Twists and Turns!

Looking above at fallen leaves tinged with brown beauty, as they

Twist and turn on their perilous journey like First World War soldiers, to

The ground, some adventurous gliding through the air, like a silent owl

At dusk, and others tumbling as if their appointed time has come, letting go

Of their golden place for so long, guardians of majesty, a whirlwind of change

Small and yet significant, many and yet individual, as if stirred this autumn day

To resonate a picture hidden of a season coming to an end!

Solitary Opportunists!

Solitary Crows, in the bleak, unrelenting rain, moving
Purposefully for rich pickings on the sodden field, of
Past Torment, conflict long since dimmed, other than
Lowly earth works, bastions of musket fire, trodden on
By these searching, seeking birds of earlier Viking doom,
Yet nothing deters them from what they need to do!

Trees of Life

Bastions of strength, blowing so freely in the Saharan air, flowing
With life, backwards and forwards, displaying such vitality above
The estuary fresh, breathing inspiration into our weakened Spirits,
As we hear and feel the hidden mystery of bracing boughs, dancing
With the summer wind!

The Wood Pigeon

Sheltering below the low bush ridge on this
Windblown headland, cold biting wind stirs
Shivering movements from your body as you
Crouch in stillness, suddenly to move slowly
To feed on whatever you can, on pavement
Bare, feathers furrowing, as you stoop again
In fearful cold, Oh for quiet woodland, sunshine
And shelter and cooing contentment! No one
Notices your presence hidden like pain within!

Devotion

Holding her terrier dear, looking
Outwards into the cold bare wind and
Rain, the safety and warmth of her
Car provides a little solace as she awaits
Patiently, looking endearingly to myself
And Sidney outside, as if a younger self
Is still within her, her shawl and stick
Helping her through, crouched acute,
She battles uphill in love and devotion!

Awakened!

Quiet interlude, unrushed, resting
In smooth meanders, glistening on
The silver surface of the sea, midges
Rising in the morning haze, awakened
As we are by the warmth of a son!

The Whistling Wind!

There is such harmony as the wind blows over the sea, the
Trees, and the ferns, their flow of life and interaction has
A message that I miss, looking seawards from estuary edge
As sailing yachts whisp forward in the soothing breeze, there
Peaceful images merge with the wood pigeon's call, and buzzing
Bees, creating a balm to bring to rest the constant daily
Messages from my mind and open to me a peace beyond!

The Empty Bottle!

Empty plastic bottle rolling down the hill, blowing
Left and blowing right, aimlessly, at the will and mercy
Of the wind, as if you have no direction other than where
You are taken, your sounds resonate so hauntingly into
My soul, as you come to rest, and I can think at last!

The Sleeping Street!

A lady drops dog waste into the street bin, the lid closes
As she passes quietly by, and this solitary sound breaks the silence
Of the deserted street, as if everyone is asleep, cars carefully
Parked alongside the cottage houses, no human voice is heard, only
The silent steps after moments of stillness, of another lady who walks
By with her collie, occasional cars pass after some while, and the
blooms of colorful hanging baskets speak their own language, as
the running water in medieval leats sooth in motion, our hurried
lives as we wait for fish and chips!

White Sails at Night!

Glistening moonlight glows on the emerald sea, softening
Our day whilst the mystery of its sparkling reflection dancing
Like the white sailed yachts whispering by, breezes a romantic
Enchantment, and beckons an intimacy we can easily miss!

Rest!

Cows swishing their tails in the mid-day sun, sitting
in welcome shade, as the oak trees gently sway, whilst
buzzing flies resonate a peaceful serenity around them,
reaching our souls, as the summer fields convey a welcome
resting place for them, and for us!

The Sycamore Trees

The wind blows wistfully through the sycamore trees, sweeping
Its mysterious beauty in innocence, invisible in its impact, as leaves
And branches move like a symphony, backwards and forwards, as if
Dancing together to the delight of a hidden orchestrator!

Winter Magic

Slipping and Sliding on snowy slopes, pictured
People painted past, like Lowry figures locked
In time, leased fields to winter's bitter chill,
yet laughter, Joy, Simplicity of Fun, releases hearts, to
See beyond the fractured falseness of human being
Necessary perhaps, but a deeper depth presents,
As toboggans speed, all ages talk and play, under
The falling snowflakes, without cost or charge, or
"Interest free," save freezing toes and finger tips
Which come as quickly as they go!

Echoes of the Norsemen!

Looking seaward eerie oars rocking backwards and forwards
In early-morning mist, sounding like distant Norsemen coming
Ever closer, creaking wood pounding as arm muscles move in
Methodical might, guided onwards, as rhythmic sounds stretch
Across the estuarine mouth, focusing our attention peacefully
Unlike those of long ago!

Unexpected Gift!

Joyful laughter as Sidney in darkened mystery brings
His emergent love into hidden lives, staring at the whitened
Waves, the young couple receive our puppy's interest
And warmth, expressed in bodily touch as he wanders in between
Them, brushing his softened coat by their side, bringing to them an
Unexpected gift!

The Washing Line

Washing blows so innocently in the wind, whistling
and swaying, as if it carries itself through time, like
an innocent sentinel, or empty swing in sadness, drying
in the warm, whispful air, and signalling a normality
in its rhythm of our intervention with nature, using
its potential, but at its mercy, as with those people
in suffering who trust and yet cannot know!

Devotion

Beckoning hand, to a distant mystery, still
Unclear, as the rugged man, looking behind
Awaiting expectantly, moves his arm towards
What was hidden by concrete support struts, in the
Underworld of grafiti art and BMX jumps, where
Thundering traffic above vibrates, in this noisy urban
World of speeding by, whilst we simply sit and look, as
A loyal friend appears, striving and struggling to reach
Him, his three legs holding his balance, to the utmost
Limit of his endurance, with eyes glowing, fixed
On reaching his friend, his longing desire to catch
Up and be with him, moving myself and Datan,
Before he too disappears, prepared to follow him
Anywhere, through hidden brambles and undergrowth
Turning his back on society, except for this exceptional
Dog, who follows beyond all impediment, even
When Exhausted, and taken for granted,
Such was his love for his master!

The Letter Box!

Glazed sunlight streams seaward against the stretching sea,
Providing glimpses of warmth and hope where grey-toned water
Surrounds, looking skyward the narrow slit of light, beckons
Attention, as if a mysterious letter box is asking to be pushed open,
before the day moves on!

Resolve

Holding with gritty determination the shepherd's crook, battling
In frozen gaze the wind-chilled street, whist the silent movement
Of age accompanies him, observed by a neighbor who leans against
His front porch, using every ounce of strength to balance, yet within
A human resolve to move and live, as with the lady whose every uphill
Step with bag and stick, consumes her energy, as she patiently rests
    before
Her next step takes her closer to home, returning to a simplicity of
    survival!

Morning Hope!

Splayed sunlight stretching like supernatural light beams,
Piercing through cloud gaps, like a focusing lens on the seascape,
Glowing like emerald gems, conveying a glory which draws our gaze!

Wonder!

Mysterious light flames arising skyward amidst
The whistling wind, dusk's shadow casts its ever-
Emergent picture, as the castle's searchlights
Create a swirling presence beckoning
attention, where imaginary shapes patrol the
darkened line, whilst windows glow, radiating
rhythms of unreachable stories, hidden by time
itself, as we look on in wonder!

Silent Solace

Silent Solace, resonates by the haunting sound of the gate catch, abrasing

Against its metal clasp, at the whim of the blowing hilltop wind, sounding

Its sweeping presence through the towering trees, and buffeting a reassuring

Mystery into my heart, the peace and refreshing absence of intrusion, as the

Clouds move effortlessly across the channel hills, like a sand-timer sifting its

Sand silently!

The Whistling Wind

Winter wind whistling in snow-bound hills,
Biting cheeks in dusk's haven, creating its own
Silent solace, whilst I stare at the bleak, bare
Barn, stirring like a mirage; its black silhouette
Straw filled with figures far gone: a man staring
Whilst his son in previous cold invited our two
Curious dogs into his bale house, knowing a
Fragile tenderness, but for how long, as we stood
With him, his illness spreading, silently knowing
that these precious moments could live far beyond him!

The Prehistoric Water Dog (Glebe Beach)

Breathing life, the rich blue waves, with woven white spray
Shimmering inspiration into my cornered self, entering a wide
 estuarine
Mouth mediating release, as the freshened wind and sunshine,
Declare a fragrance, "Be still and know that I am God," resonating
Into my heart renewed hope, as the scampering leaves turn and
Twist on newly formed sands, creating their own dynamic dance,
While the gentle falling of autumn gold creates a gentle and moving
Message, of our own omega, yet the richness of silvery bows,
Splayed green pines, amidst yellow and orange hues, creates a cliff-
Edge splendor to enjoy our moments together, as we pass the silent
Prehistoric water dog, shaped beautifully in natural pine by the pebble
Beach, with a mottled crocodile's back of yellow, brown, and grey
Patchwork, solitary, and yet in movement, reminding our impulsive,
Logical restrictions, our minds, that sensory stimulus and imagination
Can capture God's heart!

Hope

Solitary birch, swaying in winter chill, branches
Glistening in golden sparkle, while the silent cumulus
Clouds pass by from their northern journey, effortlessly
Moving like a symbiosis of "imagery" of the intrinsic
Beauty and diversity of our lives, accompanied too by its
Hidden passing, leading us to reflect in mystery on what
Has been?
Yet perhaps in 2012, on what is to come, as
The excited expectancy of a Paralympian competitor
Passing down a station ramp, alights hope in welcoming staff
Ready to greet, lifting spirits, as her faithful companion
The Golden Labrador, sitting upright on her, seeks to serve
Whilst in dignity she powerfully conveys that we too can
Overcome, and rise beyond ourselves, as Christ showed us
2000 years ago!

December 2012

Blowing Bag

Blowing bag, you roll towards us, with the
Blustering wind, whistling through you like a
Signal of destiny, yet veiled in mystery, open
As if ready to be filled, focused, as the dancing
Wind brings you to our feet, as if you have
Something to say, before being whisked away
As quickly as you came!

December 2012.

All in a Flurry!

All in a flurry, dogs running, jumping,
Meeting, and fetching balls, On the still
Dawn mirage of a bladder wrack beach
Looking out into the endless blue horizon
Forever changing into "What is beyond?"
While the quiet Labrador, led by its
Owner, bursts into spontaneous freedom
When released from his restriction, energizing
Like a Nassau rocket taking off after count
Down, retrieving its ball in expectant hope,
While people walk quietly along the calm
Sea edge, in silent reflection, as I do, looking
Across to the mini mountains of Undulating
Rock pools, where Oyster Catchers change
Their speed like Passengers late for their
Departing train, and quietly feed in purposeful
Anonymity, seeking no recognition beyond
Their watchful winter cries, creating A beauty
Of acceptance no more or less, for what they
Were created to be!

The Hidden Brook

Warm moonlit mirage, creating a comforting glow
Amidst silent watchtowers, swaying gently by the
Timeless gurgling of nature's friend, never failing
To flow whether in winter's turbulence or summer
Trickles, creating a precious seclusion reaching into
Our hearts, whilst gazing at starlit skies' purity; in
Darkened clarity in this hidden valley, unspoilt by
Artificial intrusion, allowing a lingering of presence,
To avoid steps inside, an unwillingness to leave
Something we seek but cannot find!

Recycled Ducks (wooden replicas)

Listening in medieval anonymity, a peaceful
ambience of footsteps passing my stationary pose,
sitting Outside the courtyard café, close to the Bishops
Palace, with Lionel—our golden labrador—catching the eye
of enchanted ladies gazing, and gentlemen quickly stroking
and acknowledging, yet nearby the father and daughter engage
together, beyond what I would wish to hear, with silent coffee
cups allowing space and time to talk, of "Mum sitting with me"
while "our boxer looked on" "caring for me when I was small,"
"yet here no more"; in unspoken grief releasing the pain of hardships
now, "I'm jobless dad moving here from London,"
the tone sharpened and heightened, all that's here is "recycled
ducks," as he listens is silent pain, unspoken, of a love he
cannot bring back for his daughter, or himself, as their boxer animates
two passersby, soothing loss as they speak, while I pray silently
and something sparks as they laugh together, before disappearing
beyond the pauper's gate!

Perspectives

Mysterious blackened figure, emerging
Dynamically through the tidal edge, moving like
A dancing dog across glistening sea sand, coming
Closer, enticing curiosity, and a sense of excitement,
Where mirage and reality become blurred, before I am
Drawn to this almost supernatural apparition, curved
And swaying from side to side in playful power, stretching
Human logic to a higher release beyond the ephemeral,
A longing to meet, before the solitary pole with windblown
Sea weed emerges, blowing mystery away to marvel at what
Simplicity creates so far from what we think!

Wonder!

Twisting gently in mystery, three leaves falling
In silent ambience, floating to a leaf-filled floor,
Where silent solace rests with sunshine's glow;
Comforting warmth gleaming through woodlands
Enchantment, with yellow-brown leaves bristling
In morning breeze, while a Blue Tit darts between
Thin, lined trees, as we gaze in wonder; beautifully
Created to restore, before we too move endlessly on!

November 2010

The Airborne Mystery!

Head resting sideways, listening—
to the quiet, tranquil gurgling
of an Exmoor river; journeying
water passes my watchful pose,
illuminated by darting Grey Wagtails,
and a stationary River Trout with speckled
grey markings, creating a silent
underwater beauty, awaiting flowing nutrients,
yet spectacularly disturbed by explosive
turbulence from above, leading to an ecstatic
flurry of underwater meeting, almost shark like,
with trout appearing from every secretive hide away,
to feed on broken bread, as I tilt my head and look
to the 10-foot wall above and gaze on small arms and
legs balanced what seemed precariously on "the edge,"
happily throwing food in endearing simplicity to
the fish below, yet held in firm security by
grandfather's hands, creating a picture of interactive purity,
a symbiosis of need, natural and human,
both giving and receiving,
as Christ would desire,
yet even more a depth of His love,
which was beautiful
—simplicity—
breaking into all that seems so important

—complexity—
within my mind,
yet isn't!

May 2010

The Interlude!

Slipping, sliding, shivering cars where
Community shovels skim snow and ice,
A single car's valiant ascent, but then descent, as
We watch in our isolated convoy, awaiting
Movement from the jack-knifed lorry,
Before the gritting lorry releases endless standstill,
While these frozen ice warriors turn in unison,
With shovels standing alongside, vertically posed,
Observing change at last from snow-bound screeching,
Like silent sentinels they look, chilled in snowbound Ponsanooth,
Awaiting Aslan's breath, yet there brings human
Anonymity lost in endless self-pursuit, out to its
True beauty a simple giving to others, in the grating
Sound of shovels!

The Messenger!

Sideways munching, swishing tail
Rising steam in solitary innocence, focusing
In purity of stance, unaffected by human taint,
Eyes facing forward at one with late evening's
Moorland glow, a myriad of purple heather,
With glistening gold creating a silent companionship of
Eternal beauty, at least for now!
Where Twite, Grasshopper Warbler, and Stonechat create
A rarity of surprise on adjoining posts, while
The solitary cow conveys a deepening sense
Of contentment of place, reaching though we may not
Know it, into our own aspirations and frustrations,
Drawing a desire to "feel" at last who we really are!

The Awakening!

Gently sniffing in quiet stirrings, where a robin sings
a last outcry of soothing solace, before dusk's embrace.
My young labrador catches the gaze of the elderly lady,
bringing to life what could have been a silent passing,
sharing her joy at seeing him, she rekindles sadness at
losing her close companion, with heart felt warmth and intimacy.
"I still talk to him as if he's with me," and now I cannot
have another "since my fall"
Her zimmer frame supporting her determined and painstaking
    footsteps,
wishing to catch just a sense of "past love";
looking to stroke Lionel as he wavered behind me,
I quickly say "a rescue dog," yet in her pain, she drew
beyond herself, "well done for helping him"
before she moved peacefully into the cold winter twilight!

February 2010

The Coalman!

Servant of old, no technology has reached
those frozen hands descending
snowbound tracks, shivering in icy solitude,
back arched supporting fossilised remains
—a finite heritage from our Garden of Eden;
warming an atmosphere, still able to freeze
—bound by time-capsuled habit, to bring
respite and warmth to elderly bones
—energized as always to care for her bird life
beyond herself—refusing even a welcome
cup of tea; your focus continues in grim-
faced grit, though for how long?

The Opened Door

Storm whispering powerfully in night's orange-tinted glow, weathers

Its own haunting history within our souls, before stepping into Aslan's

Closet, a house of the departed—just for now—glowing in warm serenity

And silence, with pictures of a ginger cat, time-honored

Photographs of 1930s gentlemen in their trilbies in black and white

Mystique, of Harry (our friend and neighbor) at Falmouth Bowling

Club, and ancient prints of estuarine coastline, where sail and pastoral

Fields create a symbiosis of hidden sparkle to antiquity, conveying an
     intrinsic

beauty of life. I stare from its comfort through the opened door where
     blustering

savage reality embroils all within its grasp, yet remembering to draw
     each curtain

while lights take care of their own longevity, there is a reminder

that in the absence of Harry and Jean, a bygone era lives again!

January 2010

Being Alive

All I can hear is a dog barking, and sea gulls cry whilst
Washing blows gently backwards and forwards in the wind,
Casting its own moving shadow, like a dancing horse on the
Whitened shed door—my accompanying motive,
While I sit in this hot lunch hour on the outdoor step,
Triggering childhood memories
Of sitting contentedly on grandparents' steps,
Noticing a lawn and border roses, by a quiet road,
And enjoying orange corona,
Simplicity
While merging naturally with the present,
Like a railway siding meeting the main line,
I notice Lionel cleaning himself and resting in this serene sun spot;
Lying in quiet contentment, a powerful ambience, for current financial thorns,
Reaching to them in silent calm,
Bringing through a message I cannot articulate,
Soothing like the softening breeze on my cheeks,
Or the border fern tickling my ear,
Yet reaching deeper within me
Becomes the real joy of being alive.

The Sea Swans

Distant wings in whitened haze, heading across the wind-blown
    sea,
White-tipped waves crest again the rocky inlet;
A haven of beauty which keeps my gaze
Resistant to depart—escaping to the sweeping swirl of
Whispering wind, skimming southwards as wings emerge
Ever clearer like messengers of hope,
To land in unison
Like a silent screech of natural brakes,
Webbed feet spread in comical communion,
Before mysteriously moving like the haunting Mary Celeste
To tide's edge, heads turned landward, watchful of playful pups,
Conveying a deeper stillness to rest in heart-felt relationships
The real memories of time
Releasing all anxieties beyond ourselves to something forever blue
Unchanging
Before, like the whirring wing beats rising, we too depart!

Innocence

The flow of life moves endlessly forward, almost trapped in
Its own momentum, driven by daily survival perhaps, while
A little leaf gently twists, tinged with past maturity and courtesy
Of gravity, descending slowly downwards to its earth haven, bronzed
In autumn sun, its dignity and pose sparkle to this final resting
place, surrounded by the supportive force of underlying air, its
moment decided by the innocence of its own lifecycle, yet
powerfully has much to say on the falling of humankind, often
before their appointed time, in tragedy like poppies falling from
the sky!

January 2009

What Really Matters!

Parking innocently in the cold dark entrance of the business, that

can never run dry, a lady suddenly appeared, asking "if I can but move

for a body is soon to arrive," the chilling reminder of life's frailty resurges

like a piercing thorn, and our own mortality, though I challenge the sudden

interruption within myself, "no, not a body, but a person, departed yes, but

someone loved and cherished," a voice which would at one time distant, have

needed nurturing this Christmastide, of sparkling colored lights along the

riverside of this ancient town, bringing an inner warmth, pointing ever deeper

to the tender love of the infant child, Christ, who came to bring an everlasting

life, beyond the cold reminder which I received!

The Outstretched Hand

Smiling in simplicity, of sharing bread to playful ducks, the
Young boy gives of himself, with hand outstretched as we
Pass silently by, participating in this act of beauty, a pleasure
In youth, which is ageless too, giving beyond self which ignites
Our human spirit, though can we outstretch our hands when
Wind sweeps across our face, or even when it ripples through
In quiet contentment?

The Milkman!

Quiet sacrifice in early dawn's shiver, rattling milktops betray
Those silent steps, surprising my mother, who rises early—for me—
A giving love, preparing sandwiches, before I too depart in driving
Rain before the first birds' cry, greeted by the swirling sounds of
Swaying trees, with surging water running underneath the wooden
Bridge, walked over precious moments before, by a servant of a
Bygone age, eclipsed for convenience and efficiency, yet faintly
There hidden in darkness for those in greater need!

A World Beyond!

Wide-open sands spreading with infinite mystery into
Solitary coves, rolling green hillside contours around as I
Gaze at the timeless expanse, of this wide-open estuary
With yellow and darkened grey hues weaving a pattern
of intricacy, amidst the silence of this world beyond human
strife, spotting rain faintly sounds from grey strato-cumulus
clouds, accompanied by the insulating beauty of the gusting
wind, while the two mute swans gaze in perfect unison, across
this waterless plain, waiting for the incoming tide, symbolizing
a secret which we still betray!

Injustice

Vulnerable person. . .

Your heart cry heard, in the tenderness of sculptured bronze,

Yet met by aggression and dominance,

As two hands stretch and overpower your human needs,

which pass away like a running stream.

Tuileries Garden, July 2005

Little Blue Boat!

Little blue boat resting quietly by the silent Vendee sands,
Golden as they slither in the wind towards their Indian summer,
Only the still blue sea in this cozy quiet inlet, shows any hint of change
As it advances towards us, a little like time itself creeping up in pain,
Yet in looking through this we see thanksgiving, a deeper reality as
We journey inwards rather than escaping outwards, from ourselves
As the Atlantic northwesterly breeze comes ever closer, Changing
Our inlet into a turbulent turquoise sea!

The Golden Carpet!

The sound of scuffling through leaves of autumn gold
Resonate a beauty of simplicity, as we walk up the still
Woodland path, only a solitary blackbird's alarm cry and
Distant barking dog break into this rural tranquility, as
We view the distant Quantock Hills, rolling brown gemstones
Easing into the pastoral vale below, allowing an inner journey
To take place, releasing childhood loss in the unaffected comfort
Of an open corrugated barn, winter hay bales our resting place
Breathing winter's pure chill, as our two silent companions acquiesce
Like centaurs sitting either side, viewing the landscape from high
Vantage, as we feel the Holy Presence of Christ, returning with
Him to the place of pain, before descending in peace amongst
The yellow sycamore leaves again, splayed before us like a welcome
For a roman general returning from victory!

Welcoming Hands!

Stretching hands reaching out, and curling

Seeking intimacy

Seeking Protection

A frailty
e
x
p
r
e
s
s
e
d
through embracing stronger
yet tender hands

Wrinkled too in fine bronze, breathing
a dynamic conveyance of human love!

(Inspired by a bronze sculpture of a baby reaching out to an adult in
the Tuileries Gardens, Paris)

The Buzzing Bee!

Bumblebee, buzzing persistently to enter the cottage bedroom, as
I look out, one early May morning, resting in its warm vibrations, it
Sounds a connection of tranquility, releasing within me a simplicity
Of love, of something missed deep within, as conscious logic hides
   innocence
Like a veil!